GOTHENBURG
VACATION GUIDE
2023

The Essential and Ultimate Guide to Gothenburg's Hotels, Cuisines, Shopping Tips, Insider's Tips, Top Attractions, History, and Culture

ALFRED FLORES

Copyright © 2023, Alfred Flores

All rights reserved. No part of this publication may be reproduced, distributed, or transmitted in any form or by any means, including photocopying, recording, or other electronic or mechanical methods, without the prior written permission of the publisher, except in the case of brief quotations embodied in critical reviews and certain other noncommercial uses permitted by copyright law.

TABLE OF CONTENTS

INTRODUCTION

CHAPTER ONE:

Getting to Know Gothenburg

   Gothenburg: Quick Facts and Statistics

CHAPTER TWO:

Planning Your Trip to Gothenburg

   Best Time to Visit Gothenburg

   Visa and Travel Requirements

   How to Get There

   Getting Around

   Accommodation Options

   Travel Insurance

CHAPTER THREE:

Exploring Gothenburg's Neighborhoods

   Haga

Linnéstaden

Majorna

Örgryte-Härlanda

Vasastan

CHAPTER FOUR:

Top Attractions in Gothenburg

   Liseberg Amusement Park

   Universeum Science Center

   Gothenburg Museum of Art

   Gothenburg Archipelago

   Slottsskogen Park

CHAPTER FIVE:

Cultural Experiences in Gothenburg

   Gothenburg Opera House

   Gothenburg Concert Hall

   Gothenburg City Theatre

   Museum of World Culture

Gothenburg Botanical Garden

CHAPTER SIX:
Gothenburg's Culinary Delights
- Traditional Swedish Cuisine
- Seafood Specialties
- Fika: The Swedish Coffee Break
- Food Markets and Street Food
- Michelin-Starred Restaurants

CHAPTER SEVEN:
Hidden Gems in Gothenburg
- Skärhamn and Nordic Watercolour Museum
- Marstrand Island
- Älvsborg Fortress
- Gothenburg Maritime Museum
- Gunnebo House and Gardens

CHAPTER EIGHT:

Outdoor Activities and Nature
   Gothenburg's Parks and Gardens
   Sailing and Kayaking in the Archipelago
   Hiking and Biking Trails
   Fishing in Lakes and Rivers
   Wildlife Watching

CHAPTER NINE:
Shopping and Souvenirs in Gothenburg
   Shopping Streets and Districts
   Gothenburg Design and Fashion
   Local Crafts and Artisan Shops
   Antique Stores and Vintage Finds
   Souvenirs and Gifts

CHAPTER TEN:
Nightlife and Entertainment in Gothenburg
   Bars and Pubs
   Live Music Venues

Nightclubs and Dance Floors
Comedy Clubs and Theaters
Cultural Events and Festivals

CHAPTER ELEVEN:
Practical Information for Travelers
Transportation Options
Money and Currency Exchange
Language and Cultural Etiquette
Safety Tips
Emergency Contacts
Health and Medical Services

CHAPTER TWELVE:
Gothenburg's Surrounding Areas
Bohuslän Coastline
Gothenburg Archipelago Islands
Smögen Village
Tjolöholm Castle

Marstrand Island

CHAPTER TWELVE:

Conclusion and Farewell to Gothenburg

CHAPTER THIRTEEN:

Appendix

30 Useful Swedish Phrases and Pronunciations

Currency Conversion Chart

Packing List for Gothenburg

Top 10 Things to Do in Gothenburg

MAP OF GOTHENBURG, SWEDEN

INTRODUCTION

GOTHENBURG VACATION GUIDE 2023

Welcome to Gothenburg, the vibrant and enchanting city nestled on Sweden's west coast. In this comprehensive vacation guide, we invite you to embark on a journey through the heart of Scandinavia's second-largest city – a destination brimming with cultural treasures, captivating history, and a modern spirit that beckons travelers from around the world.

Unveiling Gothenburg's Charms

Gothenburg skillfully combines the appeal of the past with the innovations of the present thanks to its attractive canals, old neighborhoods, and a booming food scene. Every nook of the city has a special tale waiting to be uncovered, from the quaint cobblestone lanes of Haga to the avant-garde architecture of Lindholmen.

Chapter Highlights

- A Glimpse of Gothenburg:

- Uncover the city's intriguing history and how it has evolved into the cultural hub it is today.

- Delve into Gothenburg's architecture and urban planning, showcasing a harmonious blend of traditional and contemporary styles.

- Savor the Flavors:

- Embark on a culinary adventure through Gothenburg's gastronomic delights, from traditional Swedish dishes to a fusion of international flavors.

- Explore the city's vibrant food markets, where local produce takes center stage.

- Rest and Rejuvenate:

- Discover a selection of Gothenburg's finest hotels and accommodations, catering to every traveler's taste and budget.

- Learn insider tips on finding the perfect place to stay, ensuring a comfortable and memorable visit.

- Shop Like a Local:

- Navigate Gothenburg's diverse shopping districts, featuring everything from designer boutiques to vintage treasures.

- Get expert advice on the best shopping spots for unique souvenirs and fashion finds.

- Insider's Tips and Hidden Gems:

- Unravel the secrets of Gothenburg known only to the locals – hidden parks, tucked-away cafes, and lesser-known attractions.

- Maximize your experience with practical tips on transportation, safety, and cultural etiquette.

- Top Attractions:

- Explore Gothenburg's must-visit landmarks, museums, and art galleries that showcase the city's rich cultural heritage.

- Discover the best ways to experience Gothenburg's iconic landmarks, such as Liseberg Amusement Park and the Gothenburg Opera House.

- Embracing Gothenburg's Heritage:

- Immerse yourself in Gothenburg's fascinating history, from its Viking roots to its role as a major port city.

- Uncover the city's cultural gems, including art exhibitions, music festivals, and theater performances.

The above outlines and likes are discussed in this guide; you get to explore them as you open each chapter and page of this guide.

Whether you're a first-time visitor or a seasoned traveler to Gothenburg, this guide is your ultimate companion for exploring every facet of this enchanting city. From indulging in delectable cuisine to strolling through historic quarters, and from finding the perfect accommodation to unveiling hidden gems, you'll be equipped to create memories that will last a lifetime.

Get ready to embrace the captivating fusion of history and modernity that defines Gothenburg. So, grab your guidebook, pack your sense of curiosity, and prepare to experience the essence of Gothenburg in all its glory. Your unforgettable journey awaits!

Prepare to appreciate Gothenburg's intriguing blend of tradition and modernity. So gather your guidebook, pack your sense of adventure, and get ready to discover the true soul of Gothenburg. Your extraordinary journey is waiting!

CHAPTER ONE:
Getting to Know Gothenburg

Gothenburg: Quick Facts and Statistics

- **Geographical Overview:** Sweden's westernmost city, Gothenburg, is located around 400 kilometers (250 miles) southwest of the capital, Stockholm. On the mouth of the Göta älv (Göta River), which empties into the Kattegat, an arm of the North Sea, the city is strategically situated. Gothenburg is one of Scandinavia's most significant port cities and a significant center for marine trade and business thanks to its ideal location.

Gothenburg's surrounding archipelago contributes to its attractiveness and natural beauty. Numerous islands are accessible to tourists, offering a welcome contrast to the metropolitan environment of the city with their breathtaking scenery, sand beaches, and charming fishing communities.

- **Population:** According to my most recent update in September 2021, there were about 581,822 people living in Gothenburg. Please be aware that statistics on the population may have altered since then.

- **Climate and Weather:** Due to its close proximity to the shore, Gothenburg has a temperate maritime climate. The city has warm summers, with typical highs of 15°C to 20°C (59°F to 68°F), making it a great season for exploring and outdoor sports. In comparison to other regions of Sweden, the winters here are quite moderate, with average temperatures ranging from -1°C to 3°C (30°F to 37°F). However, sporadic cold snaps that bring temperatures below freezing can happen.

Visitors should prepare for showers even during the summer because rainfall occurs throughout the year. Despite this, the city's weather is notorious for being unpredictable, so it is best to be ready for unforeseen changes by packing clothing appropriate for a variety of weather conditions.

- **Industry:** Historically, Gothenburg was a major seaport and played a crucial role in Sweden's industrial revolution. Today, it remains an important center for trade, shipping, and industry, including automotive manufacturing.

- **Economy:** The city's economy is varied, with important contributions from industry, shipping, trade, technology, and tourism.

- **Landmarks:** The Liseberg amusement park, the Gothenburg Opera House, and the well-known bronze statue of Poseidon by Swedish sculptor Carl Milles are just a few of the notable monuments of Gothenburg.

- **Education:** The University of Gothenburg and Chalmers University of Technology are only two of the prestigious schools in Gothenburg.

- **Transport:** Visitors can easily explore the city's varied attractions thanks to its comprehensive public transit system, which includes buses, trams, and ferries.

- **Tourism:** Gothenburg attracts tourists from around the world who come to explore its charming neighborhoods, cultural attractions, and scenic landscapes.

- **History and Culture:** King Gustav II Adolf of Sweden founded Gothenburg in 1621, beginning the city's history. In order to challenge the Hanseatic League's hegemony in the area, the city was founded as a planned and protected commerce hub. Gothenburg developed over time into a significant port city, contributing significantly to Sweden's industrial revolution in the 19th century.

The architecture, museums, and cultural institutions of the city are clear examples of its rich cultural legacy. Gothenburg is home to a unique mix of old and modern structures, including the well-preserved Kronhuset (Crown House) and Skansen Kronan (Crown Keep). Museums like the Gothenburg City Museum and the Gothenburg Museum of Art highlight the artistic and historical significance of the city.

- **Festivals and Events:** Gothenburg is a city that enjoys partying, and it holds a wide variety of festivals and events throughout the year that draw both residents and tourists. The most well-known festivals include:

- Göteborg Film Festival: Every year in late January, this event showcases the best in Nordic and international filmmaking, attracting creators, performers, and movie buffs from all over the world.

- Way Out West: One of Sweden's most well-known music festivals, Way Out West takes place in August and boasts a diverse lineup of musical performers from rock and pop to techno and hip-hop.

- Göteborgsvarvet: The biggest half-marathon in the world is held in May and draws thousands of runners who participate in this renowned race while taking in the beautiful scenery along the course through the city and its environs.

- Christmas Markets: During the holiday season, Gothenburg changes into a winter paradise with charming Christmas markets that provide a variety of crafts, sweets, and seasonal happiness.

The robust cultural scene in Gothenburg, which embodies the city's energetic personality and passion for art, music, and celebration, is only a peek of what visitors may expect from these festivals and events.

Understanding Gothenburg's geographical environment, climate, history, and cultural tapestry can help you better appreciate this enthralling city as you travel around it. Accept the variety of experiences it has to offer and immerse yourself in Gothenburg's distinctive fusion of heritage and contemporary.

CHAPTER TWO:
Planning Your Trip to Gothenburg

Congratulations on your decision to travel to Gothenburg! We will walk you through the crucial processes of organizing your trip to this magical city in this chapter. We can help you with anything from picking the ideal time to travel and comprehending visa procedures to traveling there, figuring out the city, discovering lodging, and protecting your safety with travel insurance.

Best Time to Visit Gothenburg

The ideal time of year to travel to Gothenburg will mostly rely on your preferred activities and weather. With mild temperatures and more daylight hours, the summer season, which runs from June through August, offers the most comfortable weather. The best time of year to visit the city's outdoor attractions, go on gorgeous boat trips, and take part in festivals and activities.

Consider going during the shoulder seasons of spring (April to May) and autumn (September to October) for a less crowded experience and cheaper lodging costs. The weather is still pleasant throughout these months, and you can take pleasure in the city's parks and landscapes' shifting hues.

Temperatures drop throughout the winter months of December through February, but it's a lovely time to visit the city's Christmas markets, snug coffee shops, and winter activities.

Visa and Travel Requirements

Checking the Gothenburg visa and travel requirements according to your nationality is imperative before heading there. Sweden is a member of the Schengen Area, which dispenses visas to visitors for brief visits (often up to 90 days within a 180-day period). The Swedish embassy or consulate in your country will have the most up-to-date information, however exact visa requirements may change.

How to Get There

The major airport serving the city is Göteborg Landvetter Airport (GOT), which has excellent international connections. It offers flights to popular foreign locations and a number of

European towns. The Göteborg City Airport (GSE) also handles a few domestic and regional flights.

Alternatively, you can take a ferry from Denmark, Germany, or the UK or take the rail from nearby nations to get to Gothenburg.

Getting Around

Gothenburg's public transit system is effective and well-connected, making it simple for tourists to see the city and its surroundings. For navigating the city's core and visiting major sights, the Gothenburg tram network is incredibly practical. Buses and ferries are an addition to the public transportation network that make it simple to reach islands and nearby coastal locations.

Renting a bike in Gothenburg is a popular choice for greater flexibility and independence because the city is bike-friendly with designated lanes and rental facilities.

Accommodation Options

Gothenburg provides a variety of lodging choices to fit different needs and interests. You can choose from opulent hotels, quaint boutique inns, and affordable hostels; whichever suits your needs. Consider staying in one of the lovely hotels or guesthouses on the archipelago islands for a distinctive experience. Here are some popular accommodation options in Gothenburg:

- Hotels: Gothenburg boasts a wide selection of hotels, catering to various budgets and tastes. Luxury travelers can indulge in upscale hotels that offer top-notch amenities, stunning views, and exceptional service. Mid-range hotels provide a comfortable stay with modern facilities, while budget hotels offer affordable options without compromising on quality.

- Hostels: Ideal for backpackers and budget-conscious travelers, hostels in Gothenburg provide affordable accommodation in shared dormitories or private rooms. Many hostels offer communal spaces, kitchens, and social activities, making them an excellent choice for meeting fellow travelers and exchanging experiences.

- Guesthouses and Bed & Breakfasts: For a more intimate and homey experience, consider staying in a guesthouse or bed & breakfast (B&B). These accommodations are often run by locals, providing a personalized touch and insider tips on the best places to visit in Gothenburg.

- Airbnb and Vacation Rentals: Airbnb and other vacation rental platforms offer a range of apartments, houses, and studios, giving travelers a chance to experience Gothenburg like a local. Renting a vacation home can be an excellent choice for families or groups who prefer the flexibility of cooking and living like a resident.

- Boutique Hotels: Gothenburg boasts several boutique hotels that stand out for their unique design, character, and attention to detail. Staying in a boutique hotel adds a touch of charm and individuality to your accommodation experience.

- Floating Hotels: Given its maritime heritage, Gothenburg also offers the unique experience of staying in floating hotels and hostels, located on boats and ships. This option is perfect for those seeking a memorable and immersive stay on the city's waterways.

Regardless of the accommodation type you choose, it's advisable to book in advance, especially during peak tourist seasons or major events to secure the best rates and availability. Additionally, many accommodations offer free cancellation policies, providing flexibility for changes in your travel plans.

No matter where you stay in Gothenburg, you'll be able to enjoy the city's vibrant atmosphere, friendly locals, and a wealth of attractions and activities. Whether you're exploring the picturesque canals, visiting museums and galleries, or savoring delicious Swedish cuisine, Gothenburg's accommodation options will enhance your overall travel experience.

Travel Insurance

It is crucial to remember to purchase travel insurance while making travel arrangements. It offers financial security against unanticipated occurrences including trip cancellations, illness, misplaced luggage, and travel delays. Examine the policy's provisions for medical costs, repatriation, and coverage for the activities you want to engage in carefully before buying travel insurance.

With a well-thought-out itinerary and practical considerations taken into account, you can confidently start your adventure in Gothenburg. Gothenburg guarantees a memorable experience, whether you choose to explore the city's historical sites, indulge in its gastronomic offerings, or simply take in the tranquility of its natural surroundings. Travel safely!

CHAPTER THREE: Exploring Gothenburg's Neighborhoods

The city of Gothenburg is home to a variety of neighborhoods, each with its own unique charm and personality. Three of the city's most cherished districts—Haga, Linnéstaden, and Majorna—are the subjects of this chapter's in-depth examination. These neighborhoods provide distinctive experiences that will enhance your trip to Gothenburg, from historical sites and cultural landmarks to chic stores and buzzing cafés.

Haga

One of the most recognizable areas of Gothenburg is Haga, which is known for its beautifully maintained 19th-century architecture, cobblestone streets, and welcoming ambiance. Haga, which is a popular destination for both locals and tourists, is a short stroll from the city center and is known for its lovely boutiques, antique shops, and cozy cafés.

Highlights of Haga include:

- Haga Nygata: Lined with vibrant wooden buildings, cafes, and stores, Haga Nygata is the city's main thoroughfare. Explore the distinctive businesses providing everything from fashion to interior design while taking a leisurely stroll down this gorgeous boulevard.

- Haga Church: A notable landmark in the area, this lovely neo-gothic church is worth a visit to appreciate its design and tranquil settings.

- Café Culture: Haga is well-known for its thriving café scene, and you'll find a ton of cafes serving delectable pastries, coffee, and traditional Swedish sweets like cinnamon buns (kanelbullar). Take a fika (coffee break) at one of the quaint places and take in the atmosphere of the neighborhood.

Linnéstaden

Known for its blend of contemporary city living and open spaces, Linnéstaden is a bustling and diverse neighborhood. This neighborhood, which bears the name of renowned Swedish botanist Carl Linnaeus, is distinguished for its broad boulevards, attractive structures, and lush parks.

Highlights of Linnéstaden include:

- Slottsskogen Park: Located in the center of Linnéstaden, this sizable urban park is a beloved haven. Slottsskogen provides chances for picnics, jogging, and relaxation thanks to its meadows, woodlands, petting zoo, and playground.

- Linnégatan: Linnégatan, the bustling street that runs through Linnéstaden and is lined with eateries, pubs, and shops. It's a fantastic location to sample Gothenburg's cutting-edge food scene and exciting nightlife.

- Götaplatsen: The City Theatre, the Gothenburg Museum of Art, and the statue of Poseidon are all located in this important Linnéstaden square. It's a center for culture where you may go to shows or just take in the creative atmosphere of the city.

Majorna

Majorna is a stylish and trendy area that draws a variety of people to it thanks to its artistic atmosphere, unique stores, and vibrant music scene. Majorna, which was formerly an industrial district, has evolved into a creative hub that captures the essence of the modern, forward-thinking city.

Highlights of Majorna include:

- Mariaplan: The bustling Mariaplan square in the center of Majorna is home to a farmers' market, cafes, and restaurants. Locals frequently congregate there, and you may experience the lively atmosphere of the area.

- Art and Music: Majorna is well renowned for its thriving arts and music culture, with many galleries and music venues featuring both local and international talents.

- Slottsskogen and Älvsborg Bridge: Although Slottsskogen technically stretches into Majorna, it is a well-liked vacation spot for outdoor enthusiasts despite being a part of Linnéstaden. Additionally, Majorna is connected to the island of Hisingen by the charming Älvsborg Bridge, which provides breathtaking views of the city.

Örgryte-Härlanda

East of the city center is the tranquil neighborhood of Örgryte-Härlanda. This area is renowned for its tranquil environment, huge green spaces, and old structures. It offers the ideal compromise between urban living and serene natural surroundings, making it a desirable location for people looking for a peaceful getaway from the busy metropolis.

Highlights of Örgryte-Härlanda include:

- Liseberg Gardens: While officially extending into Örgryte-Härlanda, the Liseberg Gardens are actually a component of the nearby Liseberg amusement park. This picturesque park provides strolling paths, immaculate gardens, and a nice café, offering a peaceful escape for both tourists and locals.

-- Skatås: Skats: For outdoor aficionados, this natural preserve and recreation area is a refuge. Skatås is the ideal location for leisurely walks or energetic sports amidst the beauty of nature because it has hiking trails, running lanes, and a sizable lake.

- Örgryte Church: This magnificent specimen of Gothic Revival architecture is a well-known landmark in the area. For those who enjoy architecture, it is a sight to behold and a fascinating place to visit because of its tall spires and intricate exterior.

Vasastan

Vasastan, a bustling and contemporary district in the northern part of Gothenburg, stands out for its creative flare, bright street art, and variety of cafés and eateries. Vasastan has established itself as a favored hangout for musicians, artists, and young professionals thanks to its artistic vibe and bohemian atmosphere.

Highlights of Vasastan include:

- Street Art: Vasastan has a thriving street art community, with colorful murals covering many of the city's structures. Explore the streets on your own or join a street art tour to find these fascinating urban creations.

- Victoriapassagen: Victoriapassagen offers a distinctive shopping experience for fashion fans and collectors with its attractive pedestrian passageway lined with boutiques, vintage stores, and cafés.

- Café and Music Scene: Vasastan is a hotspot for trendy cafés and live music venues, making it the perfect area to spend a laid-back afternoon with delicious coffee and live music.

- Ramberget: This hill provides sweeping views over Gothenburg and the surrounding area, making it a well-liked location to take in the city's skyline and breathtaking sunsets.

You will gain a deeper grasp of Gothenburg's complex identity by exploring these neighborhoods. You can learn something new about the history, culture, and modern way of life of the city in each location, adding to the richness and significance of your trip to Gothenburg. So get out there and enjoy the variety and inventiveness that these three fascinating communities have to offer.

CHAPTER FOUR:
Top Attractions in Gothenburg

Gothenburg is home to numerous captivating attractions for people of all ages and interests. This chapter will examine the Liseberg Amusement Park, the Universeum Science Center, and the Gothenburg Museum of Art, three of the city's most well-known and cherished landmarks. Each site provides a distinctive experience that showcases the city's thriving arts, entertainment, and culture scenes.

Liseberg Amusement Park

The largest amusement park in Scandinavia, Liseberg, is a cherished Gothenburg landmark. The 1923-founded park has grown into a sizable entertainment complex with a wide selection of rides, attractions, shows, and seasonal events. Liseberg is the perfect vacation spot for families, thrill-seekers, and culture fans alike because it offers something for everyone.

Key highlights of Liseberg Amusement Park include:

- Roller Coasters: Liseberg is well-known for its thrilling roller coasters, which give thrill-seekers a heart-pounding sensation. You can be sure that rides like Helix, Balder, and Valkyria will make your heart race.

- Gardens and Landscapes: Liseberg is home to thrilling rides in addition to exquisitely landscaped gardens that offer a tranquil getaway for those looking to take a leisurely stroll through the outdoors.

- Seasonal Festivals: Liseberg organizes festivals and events throughout the year, including the well-known Christmas market in the winter and Halloween celebrations in the fall. These activities give the park a festive feel and give visitors a sense of wonder.

- Entertainment: The park hosts live performances, concerts, and other events all year long, guaranteeing that there is always something fun to take in.

Universeum Science Center

A state-of-the-art science facility, Universeum mixes learning with enjoyment and interactive experiences. One of the most cutting-edge and interactive science museums in Scandinavia, it takes visitors on a fascinating tour of many scientific fields and the natural world. Universeum is a stimulating experience that promotes a deeper understanding of our world and the universe, making it ideal for families and inquisitive minds.

Key highlights of Universeum Science Center include:

- Rainforest Exhibition: This eye-catching exhibit of exotic plants and fauna features an outstanding indoor rainforest. Visitors can discover the rainforest's numerous levels, discover its ecosystems, and interact with a variety of tropical animals.

- Ocean Zone: The Ocean Zone has aquatic ecosystems and marine species, allowing visitors to get up close and personal with marine life while also learning about the value of ocean conservation.

- Space Exhibition: Investigate the mysteries of the cosmos at this interactive exhibit that also includes planetarium shows and space probe models.

- Health and Body: Universeum Universeum also emphasizes these topics, with exhibits that explore the complexity of the human body and advocate for healthy living.

Gothenburg Museum of Art

The Gothenburg Museum of Art, one of Sweden's most prestigious art institutions, is home to a significant collection of Swedish and foreign works of art from the 15th century to the present. Impressionism, Post-Impressionism, and Nordic Romanticism are just a few of the many art movements represented in the museum's extensive and varied collections.

Key highlights of the Gothenburg Museum of Art include:

- Nordic Art Collection: The museum is home to a sizable collection of Nordic art, which includes pieces by well-known Swedish artists including Anders Zorn, Carl Larsson, and Bruno Liljefors.

- French Art: The museum's collection is notable for its array of 19th- and 20th-century French artwork, which includes pieces by Claude Monet, Édouard Manet, and Henri Matisse, among others.

- Temporary Exhibitions: The museum presents temporary exhibitions that highlight contemporary art and introduce guests to up-and-coming artists in addition to its permanent collection.

- Architectural Beauty: With its beautiful neo-classical design and eye-catching marble staircase, the building is in itself a work of art and serves as the perfect backdrop for the remarkable artwork it houses.

Gothenburg Archipelago

A magnificent group of over 20 islands and islets dispersed along the city's shoreline makes up the Gothenburg Archipelago. This charming archipelago is a well-liked location for day visits or longer holidays because it is conveniently located from the city core. Each island in the archipelago has its own distinct attractiveness and charm, providing visitors with a wide variety of experiences.

Key highlights of the Gothenburg Archipelago include:

- Island Hopping: Travel between the many islands by using a frequent ferry. This will allow you to see a variety of topography, from rocky shorelines to sandy beaches and dense forests.

- Nature Activities: With options for hiking, cycling, fishing, and birdwatching, the archipelago is a sanctuary for nature lovers. The islands' varied scenery accommodate a range of interests and physical abilities.

- Lighthouses: The archipelago's numerous islands are home to quaint lighthouses that give your travels a hint of romance and marine history.

- Secluded Retreats: Several islands provide the ideal location for a tranquil escape, with accommodations ranging from charming guesthouses to warm cabins.

The Gothenburg Archipelago promises a revitalizing experience that highlights the natural beauty of the Swedish coast, whether you're looking for adventure, leisure, or a combination of the two.

Slottsskogen Park

In the center of Gothenburg, Slottsskogen Park is a well-liked green space. This vast urban park, which covers an area of approximately 137 hectares, provides a welcome respite from the bustle of the city. Both locals and tourists love Slottsskogen because it offers a peaceful location for picnics, leisurely walks, and recreational activities.

Key highlights of Slottsskogen Park include:

- Natural Habitats: The park has a variety of habitats, such as forests, meadows, and ponds, which together form a diversified ecosystem and draw a variety of animals.

- Animal Enclosures: Slottsskogen is a free-to-enter zoo that houses native Nordic species like moose, deer, seals, and penguins in animal enclosures. The zoo offers a chance to get up close and personal with these animals in roomy, realistic habitats.

- Paddling Pools and Playgrounds: The park features playgrounds and paddling pools for kids, making it a wonderful family getaway.

- Leisure Activities: Slottsskogen is a great location for outdoor pursuits like jogging, cycling, and picnicking. Locals frequently congregate there, especially on bright days and weekends.

Slottsskogen Park offers a tranquil haven in the middle of the city where you may enjoy outdoor activities, get in touch with nature, and take in the local animals. Whether you're visiting with loved ones, friends, or on your own, the park offers a haven of peace that blends with Gothenburg's vibrant urban environment.

These top Gothenburg attractions provide a thorough and holistic view of the city's culture and recreational activities. These attractions will leave a lasting impression and add an extra layer of richness to your visit to this dynamic Swedish city, whether you're looking for thrills at Liseberg, expanding your knowledge at Universeum, immersing yourself in art at the Gothenburg Museum of Art, or taking leisurely walks in Slottsskogen Park.

CHAPTER FIVE:
Cultural Experiences in Gothenburg

The city of Gothenburg takes pride in its extensive cultural past and thriving art scene. This chapter will look at five cultural events that highlight the city's enduring love of music, the performing arts, diversity, and the outdoors. These cultural treasures guarantee to leave a lasting impact on every visitor, from top-notch opera and symphony concerts to provocative exhibitions and serene floral gardens.

Gothenburg Opera House

On the banks of the Göta älv river sits the beautiful architectural wonder known as the Gothenburg Opera House, or "Göteborgsoperan" in Swedish. The Gothenburg Opera and the

Gothenburg Ballet perform a wide range of opera, ballet, musicals, and contemporary dance in this cutting-edge opera theater.

Highlights of the Gothenburg Opera House include:

- World-Class Performances: The opera house presents world-class performances by Swedish and international artists, showcasing both traditional and contemporary works that enthrall audiences of all ages.

- Opera for Everyone: The opera house is devoted to making opera accessible to a wide audience and presents special performances for families, students, and first-time opera attendees.

- Guided Tours: Individuals interested in learning more about the opera house's history, architecture, and inner workings can sign up for a guided tour.

Gothenburg Concert Hall

The Gothenburg Concert Hall (Göteborgs Konserthus), which serves as the home of the Gothenburg Symphony Orchestra, is a prominent location for symphonic concerts, recitals, and other musical events. The magnificent design and superb acoustics of the hall create an alluring environment for alluring performances.

Key highlights of the Gothenburg Concert Hall include:

- Symphony Concerts: The renowned Gothenburg Symphony Orchestra, one of Europe's top orchestras, will perform at these events, allowing you to marvel at the grandeur of classical music.

- Guest Performances: To broaden the musical repertoire, the concert hall also hosts renowned foreign orchestras, soloists, and conductors.

- Jazz and Contemporary Music: The venue presents jazz shows and contemporary music events in addition to classical concerts, appealing to a variety of musical preferences.

Gothenburg City Theatre

The Gothenburg City Theatre (Göteborgs Stadsteater) is a cultural center that presents a diverse range of theatrical productions, from traditional plays and avant-garde shows to experimental pieces by modern playwrights. The theater's varied programming showcases the city's dedication to supporting a thriving arts community.

Highlights of the Gothenburg City Theatre include:

- Theatrical Excellence: The theater is home to a number of brilliant actors, directors, and creative teams who often turn in mesmerizing and provocative performances.

- Multilingual Productions: Some productions are presented in a variety of languages to accommodate locals and visitors from around the world.

- Experimental Works: The theater is well-known for experimenting with cutting-edge theater techniques and tackling current social and cultural concerns.

Museum of World Culture

The intriguing cultural institution known as the Museum of World Culture (Världskulturmuseet) investigates the variety and connections of world civilizations. The museum works to advance intercultural communication through interesting exhibitions, interactive displays, and stimulating speeches.

Key highlights of the Museum of World Culture include:

- Global Exhibitions: The museum's exhibits range widely in subject matter, from anthropology and art to modern concerns like migration and sustainability.

- Hands-On Experiences: Interactive components in the displays invite guests to interact with cultural artifacts and investigate various viewpoints.

- Diverse Programming: The museum offers additional perspectives on diverse cultures and current issues through lectures, seminars, film screenings, and performances.

Gothenburg Botanical Garden

The 175 hectare Gothenburg Botanical Garden (Göteborgs Botaniska Trädgård) is a tranquil and entrancing green area. This botanical paradise is home to a huge collection of plants from all over the world, making it a wonderful vacation spot for individuals who love the outdoors and serenity.

Key highlights of the Gothenburg Botanical Garden include:

- Greenhouses: Take a tour of a collection of greenhouses that are home to exotic plants, such as tropical and desert species, offering a realistic experience in various climatic conditions.

- Rock Garden: This stunning rock garden displays a range of alpine plants and flowers, offering a magnificent backdrop for leisurely strolls.

- Thematic Gardens: The garden has a number of themed sections, including the Japanese Glade, Rhododendron Valley, and the Garden of the Senses, each of which gives a distinctive sensory experience.

- Arboretum: The vast arboretum contains a variety of trees and woody plants from various geographical areas, providing visitors with a picturesque atmosphere for exploration and relaxation.

Going on a voyage of exploration and inspiration via Gothenburg's cultural diversity. These cultural experiences offer the chance to immerse yourself in the various artistic and natural wonders that define this dynamic Swedish city, from the captivating performances at the Gothenburg Opera House and Concert Hall to the thought-provoking exhibitions at the Museum of World Culture and the serene beauty of the Gothenburg Botanical Garden.

CHAPTER SIX:
Gothenburg's Culinary Delights

Traditional Swedish cuisine, delicious seafood specialties, and the renowned fika cultural legacy are all harmoniously combined in Gothenburg's culinary scene. We shall examine the tastes, flavors, and cultural importance of these delectable dishes that make Gothenburg a foodie's paradise in this chapter.

Traditional Swedish Cuisine

The history and natural resources of Sweden are strongly ingrained in the country's traditional cuisine. It places a focus on straightforward, healthy foods obtained from both land and sea. You may enjoy traditional Swedish meals in

Gothenburg with a coastal twist to emphasize the city's marine history.

Key highlights of Traditional Swedish Cuisine in Gothenburg include:

- Herring: Gothenburg is well known for its herring dishes because it is a coastline city. The popular delicacy "sill" (pickled herring) is frequently served with a variety of savory sauces and sides.

- Meatballs: "köttbullar," or Swedish meatballs, are a well-liked comfort food. Regular accompaniments include mashed potatoes, lingonberry sauce, and thick gravy.

- Fish and Potatoes: Fish, especially salmon and herring, are common side dishes in Swedish cooking while potatoes are a staple of the country's cuisine.

- Smörgåsbord: A celebratory buffet of foods, including pickled herring and cured salmon as well as a variety of meats, cheeses, and salads, is known as a smörgåsbord: in Sweden.

- Lingonberries: These small, red berries are a staple in Swedish cuisine, commonly used in sauces, jams, and desserts

Seafood Specialties

Gothenburg is a coastal city and a haven for seafood lovers. Local chefs take delight in producing exquisite dishes that highlight the abundance of the ocean's fresh seafood and shellfish.

Key highlights of Seafood Specialties in Gothenburg include:

- Fish and Chips: Enjoy this traditional British dish with a Scandinavian touch. Cod or haddock, together with crispy fries and remoulade sauce, are frequent ingredients in Gothenburg's rendition.

- Gravlax: Dill, sugar, and salt are used to cure fish in this classic delicacy. The outcome is a succulent, delicious treat sometimes served with bread and mustard sauce.

- Seafood Platters: A variety of fresh oysters, prawns, mussels, crab, and other seafood specialties are available on opulent seafood platters at many restaurants.

- Lobster Soup: "Hummersoppa" is a rich, creamy lobster soup that highlights the lobster's complex characteristics and is frequently topped with a dash of dill.

Fika: The Swedish Coffee Break

Fika is a beloved practice that involves having coffee with friends, family, or coworkers. It is an integral element of Swedish culture. It is more than just drinking coffee; it is an occasion for mingling with others and indulging in delectable snacks.

Key highlights of Fika in Gothenburg include:

- Coffee: Swedish coffee is frequently provided with a side of hot water to adjust the strength to your preference. Swedish coffee is normally strong.

- Cinnamon Buns: "Kanelbullar" are traditional Swedish cinnamon buns, soft and flavorful, and frequently relished during fika with a warm cup of coffee.

- Pastries: Fika frequently contains a variety of pastries, including fruit tarts, almond cakes, and cardamom buns.

- Fika Venues: Gothenburg is home to a large number of quaint cafés and bakeries where you may fully appreciate fika.

Food Markets and Street Food

A feast for the senses with a vast variety of flavors, scents, and textures, food markets and street food are an essential component of Gothenburg's culinary scene.

Key highlights of Food Markets and Street Food in Gothenburg include:

- Fish Market (Feskekôrka): Literally meaning "Fish Church," Feskekôrka is a historic fish market located in a distinctive structure that resembles a Gothic church. Salmon, herring, lobster, prawns, and other fresh seafood are available here in plenty. The market's cafés are popular with guests who want a fast supper of freshly prepared seafood.

- Market Hall (Saluhallen): The Market Hall is a food hall that has been in operation since 1889 and provides a diverse range of locally produced products, artisanal cheeses, cured meats, and traditional Swedish treats. It's a great spot to see the city's culinary scene and shop for gifts to bring home.

- Haga Nygata: Haga's main street, Haga Nygata, is renowned for both its delicious street food selections and its quaint boutiques and cafés. You can find food trucks and stalls selling a range of delectable foods while strolling around this lovely neighborhood, including Swedish-style hot dogs, gourmet burgers, and food from around the world.

- Magasinsgatan Street: This chic street is a favorite among foodies because it is home to a wide variety of restaurants and cuisine ideas. Everything is available, from gourmet ice cream and specialty coffee shops to cutting-edge fusion food.

Michelin-Starred Restaurants

The restaurants in Gothenburg have won coveted Michelin stars for their outstanding cuisine, inventive cooking methods, and dedication to utilizing only the finest, locally obtained products. The city is home to an extraordinary culinary culture.

Key highlights of Michelin-Starred Restaurants in Gothenburg include:

- SK Mat & Människor: SK Mat & Människor, which received a Michelin star, is well known for its creative Nordic food. The restaurant emphasizes seasonal and environmentally friendly ingredients, serving exquisitely designed dishes that honor the region's culinary tradition.

- Bhoga: Bhoga, which also has one Michelin star, is renowned for its modern Scandinavian cuisine with international influences. The finest local ingredients are skilfully prepared for a fusion of flavors and textures in the chef's tasting menus.

- Sjömagasinet: This prestigious eatery received a Michelin star for its outstanding fish specialties. Sjömagasinet, housed in a historic structure near the port, with breathtaking views and a menu that emphasizes the best of the sea.

- Upper House Dining: This restaurant, which is atop the Gothia Towers hotel, has received two Michelin stars. The eatery offers a classy and sophisticated eating experience, with creative meals and beautiful presentations.

- Thörnströms Kök: Boasting one Michelin star, Thörnströms Kök emphasizes locally sourced ingredients in all of its inventive, modern cuisine. The restaurant's seasonal menus take diners on a gastronomic tour of the best flavors in the area.

Your appreciation for the culinary delights of the city will grow as you embark on a culinary journey through Gothenburg and indulge in traditional Swedish cuisine, mouthwatering seafood specialties, the beloved tradition of fika, market exploration, delicious street food, and fine dining. Your trip to Gothenburg will be a fascinating journey of taste and heritage if you embrace the robust flavors and cultural significance of these culinary encounters.

CHAPTER SEVEN:
Hidden Gems in Gothenburg

The city of Gothenburg is well recognized for its iconic landmarks and cultural highlights, but it also contains a number of undiscovered jewels that provide uncommon and off-the-beaten-path experiences. This chapter will focus on five undiscovered gems in and around Gothenburg: Skärhamn and the Nordic Watercolor Museum, Marstrand Island, Älvsborg Fortress, Gothenburg Maritime Museum, and Gunnebo House and Gardens. These locations offer an insight into the area's history, art, maritime heritage, and natural beauty, making them essential stops for interested tourists looking to explore Gothenburg's less-traveled areas.

Skärhamn and Nordic Watercolour Museum

In the vicinity of an hour's drive from Gothenburg, on the island of Tjörn, is the quaint fishing community of Skärhamn. This picture-perfect seaside community is well-known for its charming port, vibrant wooden cottages, and breath-taking ocean vistas. The Nordic Watercolour Museum, a cultural treasure devoted to the watercolor medium, is located in the center of Skärhamn.

Key highlights of Skärhamn and the Nordic Watercolour Museum include:

- Nordic Watercolor Museum: This cutting-edge and visually stunning museum honors the alluring world of watercolor art. It holds a number of transient exhibitions that showcase modern and vintage watercolor paintings by Nordic and foreign artists.

- Harbor Promenade: Enjoy a leisurely stroll along Skärhamn's waterfront promenade, which is studded with galleries, restaurants, and shops. It's the perfect place for relaxation and photography because of the lovely surroundings.

- Coastal Walks: Discover the stunning coastal scenery that surrounds Skärhamn. Several hiking trails offer breathtaking vistas of the archipelago and present a chance to get close to nature.

Marstrand Island

One can get from Gothenburg to the picturesque island of Marstrand in the Göta älv river by erry. This historic island is renowned for its fort, breathtaking scenery, and sailing tradition.

Key highlights of Marstrand Island include:

- Marstrand Fortress: The massive, 17th-century Älvsborg Fortress is a well-known feature on the island. Visitors can take guided tours to learn about its important strategic role and intriguing history.

- Carlstens Fästning: This stronghold is in excellent condition and gives sweeping views of the sea and the nearby archipelago. It's a great place to take in the area's coastal splendor.

- Water and Sailing Activities: Marstrand is a sailing haven, and during the summer the island comes alive with regattas and races. To explore the breathtaking seas, visitors can hire boats or sign up for sailing tours.

Älvsborg Fortress

The Älvsborg Fortress, which sits at the entrance to Gothenburg Harbor, has a considerable historical significance for the city. Initially constructed in the 17th century to defend the city from Danish incursions.

Key highlights of Älvsborg Fortress include:

- Guided Tours: The stronghold is reachable by water, and excursions provide visitors an understanding of its history and structure. The well-preserved ramparts and bastions are a fascinating trip through history.

- Stunning Views: The fortress offers magnificent views of Gothenburg port and the surrounding archipelago, making it the ideal location for photography and appreciating the surrounding scenery.

Gothenburg Maritime Museum

The Gothenburg nautical Museum (Sjöfartsmuseet) highlights the city's extensive nautical legacy and provides a detailed look at Gothenburg's seafaring background.

Key highlights of Gothenburg Maritime Museum include:

- Historical Exhibits: The museum's exhibits include ship models, navigational tools, and artifacts that provide visitors a thorough appreciation of the city's nautical past.

- Gothenburg's Shipping Industry: Learn about the development of Gothenburg's shipping sector, which was essential to the transformation of the city into a significant port.

- Interactive Features: The museum has interactive exhibits, making it a fun and educational trip for everyone who visits.

Gunnebo House and Gardens

Just south of Gothenburg sits the opulent estate known as Gunnebo House. This superbly kept-up property features a grand mansion, extensive grounds, and a quaint café.

Key highlights of Gunnebo House and Gardens include:

- Stately Architecture: The home offers a look at 18th-century neoclassical architecture and provides insight into the way of life of the Swedish nobility.

- Lavish Gardens: With walking trails, fountains, and vivid flowerbeds, the well-kept gardens around Gunnebo House are a treat to explore.

- Café and Organic Farm: The estate's café serves delectable snacks and meals created with fresh, organic ingredients derived from the property's farm.

You can escape the masses and delve into Gothenburg's lesser-known treasures by discovering these hidden gems. From the cultural offerings of the Nordic Watercolour Museum and the historical allure of Marstrand Island and Älvsborg Fortress to the maritime heritage at Gothenburg Maritime Museum and the tranquility of Gunnebo House and Gardens, each destination contributes to a well-rounded and enriching visit to this captivating Swedish city.

CHAPTER EIGHT:
Outdoor Activities and Nature

Gothenburg's scenic surroundings and varied landscapes make for the ideal setting for a variety of outdoor pursuits and nature encounters. Gothenburg has plenty to offer everyone, whether you're looking for tranquility in verdant parks, the excitement of sailing in the archipelago, or the adventure of hiking and biking routes. This chapter examines the city's outdoor pastimes and eco-friendly activities, allowing you to fully appreciate the breathtaking scenery and diverse wildlife of the area.

Gothenburg's Parks and Gardens

Gothenburg is well-known for having a lot of parks, gardens, and other open areas. These urban havens offer a chance to get away from the city and get in touch with nature.

Key highlights of Gothenburg's Parks and Gardens include:

- Slottsskogen Park: Slottsskogen is the biggest park in the city and has a zoo, a number of walking routes, and other recreational spaces. It's a well-liked location for family outings, jogging, and picnics.

- The Gothenburg Botanical Garden: This sizable botanical garden features a wide range of plant species, as well as a stunning rock garden, greenhouses with tropical and desert plants, and themed gardens.

- Trädgårdsföreningen: The Garden Society of Gothenburg is a wonderfully designed park from the 19th century. It has beautiful ponds, fountains, and a rose garden.

- Keillers Park: This tranquil park offers sweeping views of the city and the surrounding area from its hilltop location. It's the perfect location for leisurely strolls and watching sunsets.

Sailing and Kayaking in the Archipelago

With its alluring beauty and sailing options, the Gothenburg Archipelago attracts water sports lovers. In the archipelago, sailing and kayaking are unforgettable activities that let you discover secluded coves, rocky islets, and serene harbors.

Key highlights of Sailing and Kayaking in the Archipelago include:

- Sailing Excursions: A number of Gothenburg-based businesses offer sailing excursions that may be tailored to suit a range of tastes, from day trips to lengthy voyages that explore a number of islands.

- Kayak Rentals: You may rent kayaks in Gothenburg or right on some of the islands in the archipelago. Paddle in seas that are crystal clean while taking in the coastal beauty.

- Island Hopping: The archipelago is home to several lovely islands, each with its own personality and charms. Hop across islands to experience each one's distinct beauty and tranquility.

Hiking and Biking Trails

There are many hiking and bike routes in the areas surrounding Gothenburg, giving visitors the chance to get up close and personal with the area's natural wonders.

Key highlights of Hiking and Biking Trails include:

- Delsjön Nature Reserve: The Delsjön Nature Reserve offers a network of trails that meander through lush forests and around scenic lakes. It is located just outside of Gothenburg.

- Bohusleden: The Bohusleden trail is a long-distance hiking route that spans more than 370 kilometers and offers breath-taking views as it travels through various regions.

- Särö Västerskog: This nature reserve, which is located on the southern suburbs of Gothenburg, has hiking trails that pass by sandy beaches and coastal woods.

- Mountain Biking: For those who enjoy mountain riding, there are trails in places like Ale, Herkulesgården, and Sandsjöbacka.

Fishing in Lakes and Rivers

The lakes and rivers of Gothenburg offer many opportunities for anglers to throw their hooks in search of a variety of fish species.

Key highlights of Fishing in Lakes and Rivers include:

- Göta älv River: The Göta älv River offers opportunities for fishing, particularly for species like salmon, sea trout, and pike. The Göta älv runs through Gothenburg.

- Lakes: Nearby lakes including Delsjön and Aspen are well-known for their tranquil settings and fishing opportunities.

- Fishing Permits: Before casting your line, it's important to verify local laws since fishing permits may be necessary depending on the region.

Wildlife Watching

Wildlife abounds in Gothenburg's natural settings, offering fantastic chances for birdwatching and spotting local species.

Key highlights of Wildlife Watching include:

- Birdwatching: Several species of migratory and seabirds frequent the islands in the Gothenburg Archipelago, making it an excellent location for birdwatching.

- Nature Reserves: Explore nature reserves like Hovås Kile, Vättlefjäll, and Säveån, where you may spot local wildlife, including deer, foxes, and a variety of bird species.

- Seal Safaris: Several companies in the archipelago provide seal safaris, which let you see these endearing marine mammals in their natural environment.

Gothenburg is an area of remarkable beauty, abundant biodiversity, and a strong connection to the surrounding landscapes and waters. As you immerse yourself in outdoor activities and nature experiences there, you'll learn this for yourself. Each excursion promises to be an unforgettable and enriching journey into the heart of Gothenburg's natural treasures, whether you choose to explore parks and gardens, sail in the archipelago, hike through forests, fish in lakes and rivers, or watch wildlife.

CHAPTER NINE:
Shopping and Souvenirs in Gothenburg

Gothenburg has a busy and varied shopping culture with a mix of contemporary commercial streets, fashionable neighborhoods, and neighborhood handicraft stores. Gothenburg has something to satisfy every shopper's tastes, whether they are looking for hip Scandinavian designs, unusual mementos, or traditional Swedish crafts. We'll look at the city's shopping areas, design and fashion options, and locations for local artisan and craft stores in this chapter.

Shopping Streets and Districts

Gothenburg has a number of shopping avenues and areas that may accommodate all tastes and price ranges. In addition to being fantastic for shopping, these locations also provide a lovely ambiance and possibilities for people-watching.

Key Shopping Streets and Districts in Gothenburg include:

- Avenyn (Kungsportsavenyn): Lined with stores, eateries, and cafes, Avenyn is Gothenburg's major thoroughfare. It's a dynamic and busy region that's ideal for shopping for clothes and taking in the energetic atmosphere of the city.

- Magasinsgatan: In the heart of the city, this fashionable street is home to independent boutiques, design shops, and concept stores. It is a mecca for oddball presents and distinctive fashion items.

- Nordstan: Nordstan is the biggest retail center in Scandinavia and is home to several national and international companies. It is a one-stop shop for accessories, apparel, electronics, and more.

- Linnégatan: Located in the Linnéstaden district, Linnégatan features a variety of vintage and second-hand shops, making it ideal for people looking for unique clothing and accessories.

Gothenburg Design and Fashion

Gothenburg, a city known for its design and fashion industry, presents a plethora of chances to discover chic, modern Scandinavian designs.

Key highlights of Gothenburg Design and Fashion include:

- Local Designers: Gothenburg is home to a large number of creative local designers who produce clothing, jewelry, and home goods that capture the minimalist and modern style of the city.

- Boutiques and Concept Stores: Dispersed around the city, boutique shops and concept stores present cutting-edge designs and exclusive collections.

- Gothenburg Design Stores: Explore design-focused stores in Gothenburg that offer a curated variety of Scandinavian design goods, including furniture, lighting, textiles, and home décor.

Local Crafts and Artisan Shops

Gothenburg is a treasury of artisan stores and craft markets for anyone looking for genuine Swedish souvenirs and locally made goods.

Key highlights of Local Crafts and Artisan Shops include:

- Haga District: Haga is a historic neighborhood well-known for its quaint cobblestone alleys and artisanal stores. You can find a wide variety of locally manufactured crafts, handmade goods, and souvenirs here.

- Handicrafts and Souvenirs: Visit shops that specialize in traditional Swedish goods like Dala horses, wooden toys, glassware, and textiles to pick up some mementos of your trip to Sweden.

- Art Galleries: You can find one-of-a-kind artwork and handcrafted goods in Gothenburg's art galleries, which frequently showcase works by regional artists and craftspeople.

- Craft Markets: Keep an eye out for craft markets and fairs, which occasionally take place all over the city and provide a chance to speak with regional artisans and buy their one-of-a-kind items.

Consider looking for the "Hantverk" (craft) sign when shopping in Gothenburg to know that the store or item is made with true Swedish craftsmanship. Explore your local markets and seasonal festivals as well, as they frequently feature a variety of handmade goods and regional specialties.

Antique Stores and Vintage Finds

Gothenburg is a veritable gold mine of antique shops and vintage boutiques for collectors of antiques and items from bygone eras. These undiscovered treasures provide a chance to take a nostalgic trip through time and learn about interesting historical details.

Key highlights of Antique Stores and Vintage Finds include:

- Antikhallarna: This indoor market in the center of Gothenburg is home to a variety of antique stores and vintage retailers. Explore a diverse selection of collectibles, vintage clothing, home decor, and furnishings here.

- Second-Hand Shops: Gothenburg has a vibrant second-hand culture, with a variety of vintage and thrift shops selling previously owned clothing, accessories, and home furnishings.

- Antique Fairs and Events: Keep an eye out for local antique fairs and vintage markets where dealers congregate to display their collections and collectors can locate valuable and uncommon items.

Souvenirs and Gifts

Gothenburg provides a wide range of possibilities that capture the cultural history and contemporary charm of the city when it comes to finding the ideal presents and souvenirs.

Key highlights of Souvenirs and Gifts include:
- Swedish Delicacies: Swedish delicacies are available at local food markets and specialty shops, and include items like lingonberry jam, smoked salmon, Swedish chocolate, and crispbread. These are fantastic presents for food lovers.

- Gothenburg Merchandise: Look for trinkets that include recognizable images of Gothenburg, such as the Poseidon statue, the Liseberg amusement park, or the Paddan sightseeing boats. Tourist shops frequently sell T-shirts, mugs, and postcards.

- Dala Horses and Wooden Crafts: The Dala horse is a classic wooden horse sculpture from Sweden that is frequently decorated with elaborate paintings. For lovely gifts and decorations, look for Dala horses and other wooden crafts.

- Design and Art Prints: Numerous art prints and posters with contemporary Swedish designs and graphics are available from neighborhood art galleries and design boutiques. These prints are wonderful mementos to take home that showcase the artistic flair of Gothenburg.

- Jewelry and Accessories: Look through local jewelry shops for one-of-a-kind pieces created by regional designers, frequently with inspiration from Scandinavian aesthetics and nature.

Consider visiting tourist information offices, museum gift shops, and specialty souvenir stores when looking for presents and souvenirs because they frequently have a curated selection of things that highlight the best of Gothenburg's culture and legacy.

In conclusion, the shopping environment in Gothenburg is as varied and alluring as the city itself. Every visitor will have a wonderful shopping experience in the city, which provides everything from crowded retail areas to upscale design boutiques and lovely artisan shops. Gothenburg offers a wide range of possibilities to satisfy your shopping needs, whether you're looking for contemporary Scandinavian clothing, regional crafts, or genuine Swedish souvenirs. Furthermore, Gothenburg provides a wide range of possibilities to locate the ideal souvenir of your trip to this fascinating Swedish city, whether you're drawn to the nostalgia of antiques, the attraction of vintage clothing, the allure of Scandinavian design, or the authenticity of local crafts.

CHAPTER TEN:
Nightlife and Entertainment in Gothenburg

The nightlife in Gothenburg is active and varied, providing both locals and tourists with a wide range of entertainment opportunities. The city comes alive after dark, appealing to a variety of interests and preferences with comfortable bars, live music venues, vibrant nightclubs, and cultural events. To make sure that your evenings in the city are exciting and fun, we'll cover the various sides of Gothenburg's nightlife and entertainment scene in this chapter.

Bars and Pubs

There are several taverns and pubs in Gothenburg, each with its own ambience and menu. The city's pub culture provides something for everyone, whether you're looking for a casual evening with friends, a craft beer experience, or a chance to try Swedish aquavit.

Key highlights of Bars and Pubs in Gothenburg include:

- Andra Långgatan: This avenue is well-known for its thriving nightlife, with a wide array of bars and taverns dotting the landscape. With a wide variety of locations and venues, it's a well-liked destination for both locals and tourists.

- Craft Beer Bars: Gothenburg is known for its craft beer culture, and you can find specialty bars with a wide variety of regionally brewed and imported craft beers.

- Swedish Pubs: Take in the genuine Swedish pub environment while sampling regional beers, traditional cuisine, and the Scandinavian spirit aquavit.

Live Music Venues

Gothenburg has a vibrant live music scene that appeals to a variety of musical interests, which is great news for music fans. Live music options in the city range from small-scale performances to major concert halls, which are sure to please music lovers.

Key highlights of Live Music Venues in Gothenburg include:

- Pustervik: A well-liked location with a varied schedule, Pustervik hosts club nights, live music events, and cultural activities. It includes artists from several genres, including Swedish and foreign performers.

- Sticky Fingers: Regarded as the city's top rock venue, Sticky Fingers regularly features live performances by artists from the rock, metal, and alternative music genres.

- Gothenburg Concert Hall: In addition to hosting classical music performances, the Gothenburg Concert Hall also offers jazz concerts, world music events, and contemporary acts.

Nightclubs and Dance Floors

People looking to dance the night away to hip-hop, electronic music, and other genres can find plenty of options in the nightclub scene in Gothenburg. To accommodate various interests and dance genres, the city has a wide selection of nightclubs and dance floors.

Key highlights of Nightclubs and Dance Floors in Gothenburg include:

- Nefertiti: One of Gothenburg's oldest and most recognizable nightclubs, Nefertiti features electronic and dance music-focused DJ nights, live performances, and club events.

- Push: A well-known nightclub with a dynamic dance floor, Push plays a variety of electronic, hip-hop, and pop music to create a lively and energized atmosphere.

- Park Lane: This multi-floor nightclub plays a variety of music genres, including house and techno as well as pop and dance favorites, guaranteeing a fun-filled night of nonstop dancing.

Comedy Clubs and Theaters

Gothenburg is home to a number of comedy clubs and theaters where visitors may catch stand-up, improv, and theatrical acts.

Key highlights of Comedy Clubs and Theaters in Gothenburg include:

- Comedy clubs: Take a look at places like Stand Up Nefertiti and Ölrepubliken, which frequently feature stand-up comedy evenings with both regional and international comics.

- Göteborgs Stadsteater: The city's principal theater, Göteborgs Stadsteater, presents a wide variety of theatrical shows, including plays, musicals, and modern works.

- Improvisational Theater: Held every year in Gothenburg, Improfest is a festival of improvisational theater that attracts talented performers from all over the world.

Cultural Events and Festivals

Gothenburg is a city known for celebrating its artistic and cultural diversity through a number of annual events and festivals. There is always something spectacular going on in the city, from film festivals to gourmet events and art exhibitions.

Key highlights of Cultural Events and Festivals in Gothenburg include:

- Göteborg Film Festival: This well-known event takes place in January and features a broad range of films from many genres and nations.

- Way Out West: A well-known music event that takes place in August, Way Out West boasts a broad lineup of both Swedish and foreign performers from a range of musical genres.

- Kulturnatta: Every year, the city's cultural organizations and venues open their doors for special performances and exhibitions as part of Kulturnatta, or Culture Night, in Gothenburg.

- Christmas Markets: Gothenburg's Christmas markets provide a magical experience over the holiday season with a range of seasonal delicacies, crafts, and entertainment.

In conclusion, Gothenburg's entertainment industry and nightlife offer a varied range of possibilities to fit a variety of tastes. If you prefer live music, dancing, comedy, theater, or other cultural events, the city offers a wide range of alternatives for you to spend your nights in a vibrant and educational environment. Gothenburg promises unforgettable and enjoyable experiences that will leave you with treasured memories of your time in this vibrant Swedish city, whether you explore the bustling bars and pubs, dance the night away in vibrant nightclubs, take in live music performances, laugh at comedy clubs, or immerse yourself in the city's cultural events and festivals.

CHAPTER ELEVEN:
Practical Information for Travelers

In order to ensure a successful and pleasurable journey to Gothenburg, it is crucial to be well-prepared with useful information. The information in this chapter will help visitors traverse the city with ease and get the most out of their trip by covering crucial topics including available modes of transportation, money and currency exchange, as well as etiquette specific to the language and culture.

Transportation Options

A developed and effective public transportation system makes it simple to explore the city and its environs in Gothenburg. The primary modes of transportation are as follows:

- Trams and Buses: In Gothenburg, trams and buses make up the majority of the public transit options. You can buy single tickets or multi-trip cards from Västtrafik, which runs the city's trams and buses. Trams are a recognizable feature of Gothenburg's urban environment and offer easy access to the city's major sights and districts.

- Göteborg City Card: The Göteborg City Card provides unlimited travel on trams, buses, and boats in addition to free admission to a number of museums and attractions for tourists who want to use public transportation frequently.

- Ferries and Boats: Because of its close vicinity to the archipelago, Gothenburg also provides ferries and boats for getting around the harbor and to adjacent islands.
- Taxis and Ride-Sharing: Both taxis and ride-sharing services like Uber are commonly available throughout the city.

Money and Currency Exchange

The Swedish Krona (SEK) is Sweden's official currency. Here are some crucial pointers for monetary trade in Gothenburg:

- Credit Cards: You can use credit cards for the majority of purchases in Gothenburg, including those at restaurants, stores, and lodging facilities. American Express and other cards can be less often accepted than Visa and MasterCard.

- ATMs: You can withdraw money from ATMs located all throughout the city using your debit or credit card.

- Currency Exchange: The city's main airports, banks, and exchange offices all offer currency exchange services. Although ATMs frequently offer favorable conversion rates, you should be aware of potential bank fees when making foreign withdrawals.

Language and Cultural Etiquette

The official language in Gothenburg and all of Sweden is Swedish. Although many Swedes are proficient in English, particularly in tourist regions, it is courteous to learn a few basic Swedish words to respect the local way of life.

Here are some cultural etiquette tips for travelers in Gothenburg:

- Greetings: A polite manner to greet citizens is with a simple "Hej" (hello) or "God dag" (good day). If they are meeting someone for the first time, Swedes usually shake hands.

- Personal Space: Since the Swedes place a high value on privacy, keep a polite distance from other people when in public.

- Tipping: Compared to several other nations, Sweden does not tip as frequently. In pubs and restaurants, the bill typically includes a service fee. However, giving a modest tip as a sign of gratitude is welcomed if you get great service.

- Punctuality: Being on time for appointments and meetings is important to Swedes since they value punctuality.

- Queuing: The organized manner and respect for lines that Swedes are famed for. In queues, always wait your turn and refrain from moving in front.

- Removing Shoes: If you are invited to a private residence, be prepared to remove your shoes as it is usual to do so in Sweden.

Safety Tips

Although Gothenburg is a typically safe city for visitors, it's always a good idea to take some security measures to guarantee a worry-free trip. Here are some safety tips to keep in mind during your stay:

- Pickpocketing: Be on the lookout for pickpockets in busy areas, especially on public transit and at well-known tourist attractions, as you would in any destination for tourists. Avoid carrying a lot of cash and keep your possessions protected.

- Safer Areas: Gothenburg is thought to be a safe city for visitors, although it's best to stay in busy, well-lit areas at night. Avoid going for a solo stroll in remote locations and exercise caution when entering new neighborhoods.

- Emergency Situations: To contact police, fire, or medical aid in an emergency, dial 112.

- Drinking Responsibly: Use caution if you decide to indulge in alcoholic beverages. It is imperative to refrain from drinking and driving because Sweden has stringent rules against driving while intoxicated.

- Crossing Streets: Always use marked pedestrian crossings and watch for the green light when crossing streets. At zebra crossings, cars usually stop for pedestrians, but it is safest to wait until they have done so.

Emergency Contacts

The following emergency contacts should be at your disposal in case of an emergency while you are visiting Gothenburg:

- General Emergency: For any other emergencies, dial 112 (this number is for police, fire, and medical emergencies only).

- Police: 114 14 (For non-emergency police assistance or reporting a crime that does not require immediate attention.)

- Medical Assistance: 1177 (Healthcare advice line for non-urgent medical inquiries and information.)

Health and Medical Services

Both locals and tourists may access top-notch medical care in Gothenburg. The following are important considerations for health and medical services:

- European Health Insurance Card (EHIC): If you are a citizen of the EU or EEA, be sure to bring your EHIC so you may get the medical care you need while visiting Gothenburg.

- Non-EU/EEA Residents: It is advisable that non-EU/EEA residents buy travel insurance that covers medical costs and emergency medical repatriation because these services might not be reimbursed by Sweden's public healthcare system.

- Pharmacies: There are many pharmacies (apotek) in Gothenburg that sell both prescription and over-the-counter medicines. The "Apotek" sign should be visible, and certain pharmacies might have longer hours.

- Hospitals and Medical Facilities: Gothenburg is home to a number of cutting-edge hospitals and clinics that provide all types of healthcare. One of the biggest and most well-known hospitals in the area is the Sahlgrenska University Hospital.

- Medical Assistance: To acquire information and advice from qualified medical specialists about non-emergency medical matters, call the healthcare advice line at (877) 1177.

- Vaccinations: Before leaving for Gothenburg, inquire about any vaccines or safety precautions with the health authorities in your nation or a travel clinic.

Travelers can feel comfortable during their visit to Gothenburg by keeping in mind these useful advice, cultural customs, remaining informed about safety precautions, and knowing who to contact in an emergency. Additionally, being aware of the city's healthcare options guarantees that you'll get the support you need in the event of a medical emergency. You may thoroughly enjoy your time in Gothenburg and make priceless memories in this intriguing city by keeping these useful suggestions in mind.

CHAPTER TWELVE:
Gothenburg's Surrounding Areas

While Gothenburg has a wide range of sights and activities to offer, its surroundings are also fascinating and merit exploring. The surroundings around Gothenburg provide a variety of scenic coastal areas, medieval castles, and lovely islands, as well as a wide range of other types of natural beauty and historical significance. We'll go into detail about the top locations close to Gothenburg in this chapter, including the Bohuslän Coastline, the Gothenburg Archipelago Islands, Smögen Village, Tjolöholm Castle, and Marstrand Island.

Bohuslän Coastline

The Bohuslän Coastline, which is north of Gothenburg, is well-known for its breathtaking rocky vistas, quaint fishing towns, and distinctive nautical tradition. This coastal region, which runs the length of Sweden's western coast, combines natural beauty with cultural landmarks.

Key Highlights of the Bohuslän Coastline include:

- Fjällbacka: This charming fishing town is well-known for its red-painted cottages, sheer cliffs, and association with Swedish actress Ingrid Bergman, who owned a vacation residence here.

- Smögen: Smögen is well-known for its long wooden pier, which is surrounded by vibrant homes, seafood restaurants, and specialty stores. It's the ideal location to savor delicious seafood and the picturesque beach setting.

- Kosterhavet National Park: Kosterhavet is Sweden's first marine national park and is home to a variety of marine species, including seals and a profusion of underwater plants and animals. A nature enthusiast's fantasy is to explore the islands and beaches of the national park.

- Nordens Ark: This wildlife park is devoted to protecting threatened species from many regions of the world and offers a special chance to witness unusual animals in their natural habitat.

Gothenburg Archipelago Islands

Over 20 gorgeous islands make up the Gothenburg Archipelago, each of which has its own unique charm and attractions. These islands, which are easily reachable by boat from Gothenburg, are a haven for nature lovers and those seeking peace.

Key Highlights of the Gothenburg Archipelago Islands include:

- Styrsö: Styrsö is a well-liked spot for day vacations and restful retreats because of its lovely beaches, hiking trails, and traditional fishing cottages.

- Vrångö: The tranquil atmosphere, walking trails, and opportunities for birdwatching are well-known features of this town.

- Brännö: Brännö is the perfect island for leisure and discovery because it has beautiful nature trails, sand beaches, and delightful eateries.

- Donsö: With walking routes and stunning views of the archipelago, Donsö, an island famous for its naval heritage, is a joy to explore.

Smögen Village

One of the most well-liked communities along the Bohuslän Coastline and a must-see location for tourists exploring the area is Smögen. A lively collection of fisherman's huts, stores, and seafood eateries along its 600-meter-long wooden pier.

Key Highlights of Smögen Village include:

- Smögenbryggan: The recognizable wooden pier, Smögenbryggan, is the center of the community and a bustling gathering place for both locals and tourists. Enjoy delicious seafood dishes while strolling down the pier and admiring the vibrant homes.

- Seafood Market: Smögen is well-known for its bustling seafood market, where you can buy a variety of fresh catches, such as lobster, prawns, and fish, directly from the neighborhood fishing boats.

- Boat Trips: Explore the nearby islands, look for seals, and take in the breathtaking coastline landscape on a boat tour.

Tjolöholm Castle

The majestic Tjolöholm Castle, which is south of Gothenburg, is a fine example of English Tudor architecture from the early 20th century. The castle, which is surrounded by lovely gardens and verdant forests, provides a look into the grandeur and opulence of a bygone period.

Key Highlights of Tjolöholm Castle include:

- Guided Tours: Take a guided tour of the castle's interior to learn more about its history, architecture, and previous residents.

- Gardens and Grounds: The castle is surrounded by exquisitely designed gardens, including an English park, an Italian garden, and a rose garden, making it a lovely location for picnics and leisurely strolls.

- Events and Exhibitions: Tjolöholm Castle organizes a number of cultural events, concerts, art exhibits, and other activities all year long for guests of all ages.

Marstrand Island

Marstrand, an alluring island with a rich maritime history, magnificent architecture, and breathtaking coastline landscape, is only a short boat journey from Gothenburg. The magnificent Carlstens Fortress, positioned atop a hill and providing sweeping views of the surrounding islands and the sea, is the island's primary draw.

Key Highlights of Marstrand Island include:

- Carlstens Fortress: Visit Carlstens Fortress, a well-preserved fortress from the 17th century that has been a prison, a military outpost, and is today a well-liked historical site.

- Water Activities: Marstrand is a sailing enthusiast's paradise with options for kayaking, boat cruises, and swimming in the cool waters.

- Marstrand Regatta: Every summer, Marstrand plays host to a major sailing competition that draws competitors and spectators from around the globe for exhilarating competitions and marine events.

- Strolling through Marstrand Town: The quaint stores, cafes, and charming homes that line the narrow alleys make Marstrand Town's charming streets ideal for leisurely strolls.

The Bohuslän Coastline's spectacular coastline beauty and the Gothenburg Archipelago Islands' bucolic appeal are just a couple of the attractions found in the areas surrounding Gothenburg. Whether you decide to visit picturesque Marstrand Island, take in the lively ambiance of Smögen Village, or tour historic castles, each place promises life-changing experiences and a deeper understanding of the region's rich cultural and natural history.

CHAPTER TWELVE:
Conclusion and Farewell to Gothenburg

It's time to take stock of the educational experiences, engaging views, and gracious hospitality this dynamic Swedish city has showered upon you as your trip through Gothenburg draws to a conclusion. Gothenburg has left an enduring impression on your heart and memory, from the recognizable canals and old architecture to the vibrant cultural scene and natural beauties.

You've traveled through the quaint areas of Haga, Linnéstaden, Majorna, Örgryte-Härlanda, and Vasastan, getting a feel for the local way of life. Your days have been filled with surprise and joy thanks to the top attractions including

Liseberg Amusement Park, Universeum Science Center, Gothenburg Museum of Art, and the Gothenburg Archipelago.

The city's many cultural offerings, including the Gothenburg Opera House, Museum of World Culture, and Gothenburg City Theatre, have left you feeling inspired and a part of the area's vibrant artistic community.

Traditional Swedish cuisine, seafood specialties, and the well-known Fika coffee breaks have tantalized your taste buds and introduced you to Sweden's culinary gems.

You traveled to the Bohuslän Coastline outside of Gothenburg, where you encountered the attractiveness of fishing communities, the serenity of the Gothenburg Archipelago Islands, the historical allure of Tjolöholm Castle, and the enthralling ambiance of Marstrand Island. Your investigation of the area has gained depth and dimension thanks to these nearby areas.

You leave Gothenburg with not only fond recollections, but also a deep admiration for the city's exceptional fusion of history, modernism, and natural beauty. You have a wish to come back someday since the inhabitants' friendliness and warmth have made you feel at home.

May the experiences and lessons you learnt in Gothenburg linger with you when you go off on your next adventure, directing your explorations and influencing your perspective on life. I hope your memories of the city's energetic streets, diverse culture, and breathtaking surroundings continue to motivate and inspire you.

Farewell, dear traveler, until we meet again. May your journeys take you to far-off lands and cherished locales, but remember that Gothenburg will always have a particular place in your heart, calling you to come back and explore even more of its untapped charms. Safe travels, and may your excursions be as joyous, educational, and awe-inspiring as Gothenburg was for you.

CHAPTER THIRTEEN: Appendix

In the appendix section, we provide additional information that can enhance your travel experience in Gothenburg. Included are useful Swedish phrases with pronunciations to help you navigate the local language, a currency conversion chart to assist with financial planning, a packing list to ensure you have all essentials for your trip, and a top 10 list of must-visit attractions and activities in Gothenburg.

30 Useful Swedish Phrases and Pronunciations

Here are some essential Swedish phrases along with their pronunciations in English:

1. Hello - Hej (hey)
2. Goodbye - Hejdå (hey-doh)
3. Please - Snälla (snell-ah)
4. Thank you - Tack (tahk)
5. You're welcome - Varsågod (var-soh-gohd)
6. Yes - Ja (yaa)
7. No - Nej (nay)
8. Excuse me - Ursäkta mig (oor-sheck-tah may)
9. Sorry - Förlåt (fur-loht)
10. I don't understand - Jag förstår inte (yahg fur-storh ehn-teh)
11. Can you help me? - Kan du hjälpa mig? (kahn doo yel-pah may)
12. Where is...? - Var är...? (vahr air)
13. How much is this? - Vad kostar det här? (vahd koh-stahr deht hair)
14. I need a doctor - Jag behöver en läkare (yahg beh-hurd ehn leh-kah-reh)

15. Cheers! - Skål! (skawl)

16. I love you - Jag älskar dig (yahg el-skar deeg)

17. What's your name? - Vad heter du? (vahd hay-ter doo)

18. My name is... - Mitt namn är... (meet nahmn air)

19. Where is the bathroom? - Var är toaletten? (vahr air too-ah-leh-ten)

20. Can I have the check, please? - Kan jag få notan, tack? (kahn yahg fo noh-tahn, tahk)

21. Help! - Hjälp! (yelp)

22. I'm lost - Jag är vilse (yahg air vill-seh)

23. I'm from... - Jag kommer från... (yahg kohm-mehr fron)

24. Good morning - God morgon (gohd mor-gohn)

25. Good afternoon - God eftermiddag (gohd ef-ter-meed-dahg)

26. Good evening - God kväll (gohd kvell)

27. Good night - God natt (gohd naht)

28. How are you? - Hur mår du? (hoor mohr doo)

29. I'm fine, thank you - Jag mår bra, tack (yahg mohr brah, tahk)

30. Have a nice day - Ha en trevlig dag (hah ehn treh-vleeg dahg)

Currency Conversion Chart

Here's an updated currency conversion chart for some common currencies to Swedish Krona (SEK):

- 1 USD (United States Dollar) ≈ 9.50 SEK
- 1 EUR (Euro) ≈ 10.50 SEK
- 1 GBP (British Pound) ≈ 12.50 SEK
- 1 AUD (Australian Dollar) ≈ 7.00 SEK

- 1 CAD (Canadian Dollar) ≈ 7.50 SEK

- 1 JPY (Japanese Yen) ≈ 0.085 SEK

Please note that exchange rates may fluctuate, and it's advisable to check with a reliable financial source or your local bank for the most up-to-date rates before your trip.

Packing List for Gothenburg

When traveling to Gothenburg, consider packing the following essential items:

- Weather-Appropriate Clothing: Gothenburg experiences all four seasons, so pack clothing suitable for the time of your visit. Layering is recommended for unpredictable weather.

- Comfortable Shoes: Gothenburg is a city best explored on foot, so bring comfortable walking shoes.

- Umbrella and Raincoat: Rain showers are common in Gothenburg, especially during autumn, so be prepared with waterproof gear.

- Power Adapter: Sweden uses the Europlug Type C and F power outlets, so bring a suitable adapter if your devices have different plugs.

- Travel Insurance: Ensure you have comprehensive travel insurance to cover any unforeseen events or medical emergencies.

- Medications: If you take any prescription medications, bring enough for your trip duration.

- Travel Documents: Don't forget your passport, visa (if applicable), travel itinerary, and any other necessary travel documents.

- Sunscreen and Sunglasses: In the summer, the sun can be intense, so protect yourself from UV rays.

- Daypack or Bag: A small daypack will come in handy for carrying essentials while exploring the city.

- Travel-sized Toiletries: Carry travel-sized toiletries, including shampoo, soap, toothpaste, etc., to save space in your luggage.

- Camera and Chargers: Capture the beauty of Gothenburg with your camera and don't forget the necessary chargers.

Top 10 Things to Do in Gothenburg

As a quick reminder, here's a summarized list of the top 10 things to do in Gothenburg:

1. Visit Liseberg Amusement Park for thrilling rides and entertainment.
2. Explore the Universeum Science Center for interactive exhibits and a rainforest experience.
3. Admire masterpieces at the Gothenburg Museum of Art.
4. Discover the Gothenburg Archipelago Islands for a taste of paradise.
5. Stroll through the charming streets of Haga and enjoy Fika in cozy cafes.
6. Attend a performance at the Gothenburg Opera House or Concert Hall.
7. Enjoy fresh seafood and the scenic ambiance of Smögen Village.

8. Visit the historic Tjolöholm Castle and its beautiful gardens.

9. Explore Marstrand Island and its majestic Carlstens Fortress.

10. Experience Gothenburg's lively nightlife and cultural events.

By incorporating these useful phrases, financial planning information, packing essentials, and must-do activities into your travel preparation, your journey to Gothenburg will be enriched, well-prepared, and filled with unforgettable experiences. Enjoy your trip to this captivating city and embrace all the wonders it has to offer! Safe travels!

MAP OF GOTHENBURG, SWEDEN

Printed in Great Britain
by Amazon